How to
Preach
for a Funeral

How to
Preach
for a Funeral

Stephen K. Preus

SALM

SouthAsiaLutheranMission.com

Contents

Introduction

YOU SHOULD STRIVE FOR CLARITY in all of your preaching. When you preach certain topics unclearly, your ambiguity can become an invitation for your hearers to fill the vacuum with unscriptural ideas that supplant the divine truth. Though some people may misunderstand what you say no matter how clearly you speak, you can, so far as it depends on you, speak as clearly as you are able.

This booklet intends to aid you in this sacred task of speaking clearly when you are preaching funeral sermons in particular. To this end I will consider eight topics that I have found to be important from my own experience, and from reading and listening to pastors like my father, Pr. Rolf Preus, Pr. David Petersen, Pr. Bryan Wolfmueller, and others. While preaching on these eight topics, pastors can easily fall into a pattern of imprecision and inadvertently distract hearers from Christ and the hope we have in Him. This list is hardly exhaustive, and is certainly not an outline for a sermon, but it does include pertinent topics that pastors would do well to take note of while they are preparing funeral sermons. By focusing on these eight topics, the goal is to equip pastors better to comfort, evangelize, and catechize. Those who are attending a funeral are often more vulnerable than your average hearer, and therefore often also more attentive and receptive. Preachers should therefore make good use of the opportunity, by articulating clearly the truths of God's Word.

After addressing the eight topics below, I have appended eight sample sermons that seek to demonstrate the clarity I have striven to achieve over my years of preaching at funerals. We all have a preaching style particular to our personality, of course, and a book like this cannot fully reproduce the tone and tenor of the sermons. The content, however, is meant to be an example of how to treat these eight topics faithfully. If you find them helpful, thanks be to God. If you find them wanting, I am always willing to admit room for improvement. All of these sermons were written before this booklet was written, and I pray that you will take that into consideration as you consume and critique them. I am grateful for the sharpening iron of my brothers in the ministry and welcome your comments and questions, as together we seek to be faithful proclaimers of the faith once delivered to the saints.

This booklet originated as a workshop presentation called, "Avoiding Ambiguity and Abstractions in Funeral Preaching," which I delivered at the Bugenhagen Conference at St. John's Lutheran Church, Racine, WI, in July 2022.

1.

The Cause of Death and the Need to Preach the Law

*What is death according to people
and what is death according to God?*

Y OU MIGHT HAVE HEARD your professor of practical theology tell you that you do not really need to preach the Law at a funeral, because the Law is the dead body right in front of you. With all due respect to homileticians who have with good intention taught this in the past, I must disagree. The thought sounds a lot like the deficient phrase attributed to Saint Francis, "Preach the Gospel at all times, and use words, if necessary." The Law cannot just be the dead body, because people interpret the object lesson in lots of ways contrary to Scripture.

What is death according to people? To many, death is understood in purely medical terms. Death to them is when the doctors see the flatline and know that the heart has stopped beating. When you ask them what so-and-so died of, their answers are telling. Bob died of a heart attack. Juanita died of cancer. Delores had a stroke. They give some medical reason. All of this is true insofar as it goes, but the medical reason for death is not preaching the Law. And this medical reason for death is often all people derive from the dead body.

Other people will say that death is natural for us, just like it is for other evolved animals. They think only in terms of the circle of life. To them, the dead body in the casket teaches nothing more than that we fit into a biological cycle. This is even the case when they hear the biblical truth that man returns to the dust from which he came (Genesis 3:19). With no thought of the Life that leads to the Father (John 14:6), people look at death and think it is a part of life!

Moreover, as we know well from the rising preference for cremation instead of burial, we cannot be guaranteed even to *have* a body in a casket these days. So is there no Law with no body? Or do cremains preach the Law of God just as well? Are people thinking about God's Law when they choose to put their ground-up loved-one's flesh and bones into an urn? Is that how everyone else at the funeral would interpret it?

Obviously not. So preach death according to God. Speak of death as the punishment for sin. "On the day you eat of it you shall surely die," God said to Adam before he ate of the forbidden fruit (Genesis 2:17). "Sin entered the world through one man and death through sin," St. Paul confirms (Romans 5:12). "The wages of sin is death," he reminds us (Romans 6:23). And to connect it concretely to the Law, he writes, "The sting of death is sin and the power of sin is the Law" (1 Corinthians 15:56). Victory, he tells us, comes only from God "through our Lord Jesus Christ" (1 Corinthians 15:57). This temporal death comes about, the Law teaches, because we are by nature spiritually dead in sin (Ephesians 2:1). Without faith in Christ, this spiritual and temporal death would lead only to condemnation and the second death (Revelation 21:8), an eternal separation from God's grace and mercy.

A word of caution for how you articulate that sin causes death: Be careful to distinguish original sin and actual sins. Many people, when they hear that sin causes death, will think you are saying that God punished the deceased individual with death, because he must have committed some serious actual sin. I remember one parishioner, for example, who thought that a woman's sin of lying about him caused God to strike her dead straightaway due to her single act of deception. Although that sin alone was certainly worthy of God's condemnation, the truth of the matter is that even without this actual sin, the woman was, like everyone else, conceived and born in sin (Psalm 51:5; cf. AC II). From this original sin flow the actual sins of thought, word, and deed. This is a point worth keeping in mind.

The Law, therefore, cannot be *just* the dead body. As best as you are able, say things in such a way that the hearers cannot fit a false idea into your sermon. Otherwise, your imprecision could distract from Christ, since the hearers might not see their need for His vicarious death in their place, whereby God was "canceling the record of debt that stood against us with its legal demands… nailing it to the cross" (Colossians 2:14).

2.

Admonition Concerning Our Own Death

Is death something that only happens to others or something we should prepare for ourselves?

FOR MANY PEOPLE, THE DEATH of another does not remind them of their own mortality. It's just something that happens to *other* people. Just as they do not look at the dead body and say, "The wages of sin is death," so they do not readily say over the dead body, "That will be me one day and my wife / children / friends will be looking down at my lifeless corpse."

Instead, what *do* they say? You will hear things like, "The funeral director did such a good job with him," or "She looked so good." For better or worse, the funeral homes pretty up death with embalming and makeup to disguise the decaying of the body. They distract from the dirt and hole in the ground at the graveside with artificial grass matting. Or, as with cremation, they get rid of the body entirely so that you do not have the life-size physical reminder of a lifeless frame. Tack on the fact that few take care of the dead body themselves anymore, and it is out of sight, out of mind. Obviously, no sane soul enjoys the foulness of death; that would be morbid. By being distracted from death in so many ways, however, too many hearts are not even beginning to contemplate healthily their own death when they, one day, will meet their Maker.

So tell your hearers to prepare for death. The Lord says, "Remember that you are dust and to dust you shall return." (Genesis 3:19). Moses says, "So teach us to number our days that we may get a heart of wisdom." (Psalm 90:12). Pastors pray before the entrance of the body into the church, "Remind us that we, too, are mortal, and prepare us to fall asleep

3

in faith…"[1] We pray in the Litany that our good Lord would deliver us "from sudden and evil death."[2] When we petition our Father in the Seventh Petition to "deliver us from evil," we are asking Him to grant us "a blessed end." We sing in our Lutheran hymns, "And grant a Christian death,"[3] and "Who knows when death may overtake me?"[4] All of this is to say that we should think upon our mortality, because we want to die repentant, reconciled to those we have wronged, trusting in God's gracious promises in Christ, and entrusting our souls into our Father's hands. Too many people think a good death is just fast and painless, when they should be thinking of a death where they are prepared in faith to meet their Savior.

There is an old German prayer that puts this admonition concerning our own death into stark relief. It petitions God to remember the next person to die among those gathered and asks that he would be ready for it. Similarly, there is an epitaph found on old gravestones in our country that reads:

> Remember friends as you pass by
> As you are now so once was I.
> As I am now so you must be.
> Prepare for death and follow me.

This is not a morbid idea, but a truth worth contemplating, so that we too can die a blessed death, ready to meet our Creator, Redeemer, and Sanctifier.

Your hearers are going to die, and they need to be prepared for it. As best as you are able, say things in such a way that the hearer cannot fit his own false ideas into your words. Otherwise the hearer may be distracted from Christ, if he is not guided to cling to Him who alone delivers from death.

---

[1] *Lutheran Service Book: Agenda* (St. Louis: Concordia Publishing House, 2006), 116.
[2] *Lutheran Service Book* (St. Louis: Concordia Publishing House, 2006), 288.
[3] LSB, 689; TLH 334.
[4] TLH, 598.

3.

The Need for the Blood Atonement of Christ and Justification by Faith Alone

Is our theology "Amazing Grace" or "By Grace I'm Saved"?

Recently I met with a member upon the death of her husband. She had many Roman Catholic relatives and wanted to make sure that they heard the pure Gospel of Jesus Christ. She especially wanted them to hear that they are not saved by their works but by God's grace alone through faith alone in Christ alone. She also wanted the sermon hymn to articulate this Gospel to them. This rare occasion was a pleasant surprise, to say the least. More often you get a request to sing "Amazing Grace," a hymn that does not give a clear articulation of the Gospel.

However good (or bad) "Amazing Grace" may be as a hymn, the point is that it is vague enough to be sung by anyone who believes in a gracious god of some sort. Its unclear presentation of the Gospel, then, leads to a lot of equivocation, as each hearer gets to insert his own definition of "grace." Is this grace the unmerited favor of God (*favor Dei*) for the sake of Jesus Christ, who fully atoned for the sins of the world by His substitutionary death on the cross? Is this the grace of God that imputes Christ's righteousness to us and gives us faith in His completed work for us through the Spirit's work in His Word? Or is this grace infused into us (*gratia infusa*) and enables us to lead a sanctified life that contributes partly or entirely toward our justification before God? A sermon that makes the Gospel as ambiguous as "Amazing Grace" does could easily be understood as teaching the latter or some other incorrect idea of God's saving grace.

The member of mine who wanted a clear Gospel hymn at her husband's funeral ended up choosing "By Grace I'm Saved" for the sermon hymn.

This is our theology. Sing through it, and from your lips will come forth a hymn that clearly teaches that we are not saved by our works and conduct. Instead it teaches that God's grace is His love that sent His Son to redeem us. Grace alone brought God's Son to come do this. The Father's grace is His wide-open heart for sinners through His Son, Jesus Christ, so that though Christians know their heart's condition, they also know by faith their Savior's voice that tells them they are saved by His grace alone. Hymns like "By Grace I'm Saved," "Salvation Unto Us Has Come" and "Dear Christians, One and All, Rejoice," teach this pure Gospel clearly. Your funeral sermons should too.

In particular, articulate God's grace in the blood atonement of Christ and justification by faith alone. You know the passages. Think of how Jesus says, "The Son of Man came not to be served but to serve, and to give his life as a ransom for many." (Matthew 20:28) John the Baptist cries, "Behold, the Lamb of God, who takes away the sin of the world." (John 1:29) Saint Paul says, "We have now been justified by his blood" (Romans 5:9) and God has made "peace by the blood of his cross." (Colossians 1:20) He states that we "are justified by [God's] grace as a gift, through the redemption that is in Christ Jesus, whom God put forward as a propitiation by his blood, to be received by faith." (Romans 3:24–25a) All of this is to say, "For our sake [God] made him to be sin who knew no sin, so that in him we might become the righteousness of God." (2 Corinthians 5:21) The text you are preaching on will determine the exact wording you use, but you can employ these or other Scriptural words to make clear that Jesus actively lived in our place and fulfilled the Law for us (Galatians 4:4–5). Make it clear that Christ offered His righteous life to God while bearing the guilt and punishment of our sin by His substitutionary death (Galatians 3:13; Hebrews 2:14). Let there be no doubt that we are declared righteous in Him through faith alone "apart from works of the law." (Romans 3:28) This is a proper preaching of God's grace in Christ.

The blood atonement of Christ and justification by faith alone belong in the sermon. As best as you are able, say things in such a way that the hearer cannot fit a false idea into your words. Otherwise, the hearer may be distracted from Christ, if he has a synergistic idea of salvation instead of understanding it as a free gift of God, which is received through faith in our Savior's work in our place.

4.

The Benefits and Necessity
of the Means of Grace

*Is heaven automatic, or must faith be engendered
and nourished by the Word and Sacraments?*

UNIVERSALISM IS THE BELIEF that all mankind will ultimately be
saved. You will probably not hear people at a funeral espouse a blatant universalism, but you might hear something similar. Instead of saying that *all mankind* will be saved in the end, you might just hear that *the deceased loved one* was saved, regardless of what faith (or lack of it) he had or what life he lived. People think God must have brought their loved one to heaven, because they love this person, and so God must too. Certainly, God does love everyone in Christ. But not everyone receives His love in repentance and faith.

Some, sad to say, never receive God's love in Christ at all and were never repentant and believing Christians. Hell, not heaven, is their end. Heaven is not automatic. Hell is real, and unrepentant non-believers go there when they die. We cannot wish our loved ones into heaven, if they never knew the Way, the Truth, and the Life.

Others did receive God's love in Christ and were believing Christians at one point, yet they stopped living the life of the baptized, a life of repentance and faith in Christ, and fell back into the works of darkness. We reject the false teaching of "once saved, always saved." We also reject the Lutheran version: "once baptized, always saved." A man can lose his faith after Baptism, as Saint Peter writes:

> For if, after they have escaped the defilements of the world through the
> knowledge of our Lord and Savior Jesus Christ, they are again entangled

in them and overcome, the last state has become worse for them than the first. (2 Peter 2:20; cf. Matthew 12:45)

Saint Paul also tells us, "Therefore let anyone who thinks that he stands take heed lest he fall." (1 Corinthians 10:11–12) Clearly believers *can* lose their faith by refusing to repent and take heed to the Lord's word. Unless these people repent before they die, they end up in hell, not heaven.

Again, with something similar to a universalist mindset, plenty of people at funerals will just assume those they love had "faith" and are in heaven when they die. Heaven to them, of course, is not the beatific vision or Abraham's bosom or anything biblical. Rather, heaven to them is a place where people do whatever they enjoyed here on earth while skipping church: fishing, golfing, and so on. They cheapen faith, heaven, and our Lord by thinking this way.

Preach clearly, therefore, that faith in Christ and the heaven promised in Scripture are obtained by the means of grace, the Word and Sacraments of Christ. "Faith comes by hearing, and hearing by the word of Christ." (Romans 10:17) Jesus says, "If you abide in my word you are truly my disciples." (John 8:31) "Whoever believes and is baptized will be saved." (Mark 16:16) "Truly, truly, I say to you, unless one is born of water and the Spirit, he cannot enter the kingdom of God." (John 3:5) "Truly, truly, I say to you, unless you eat the flesh of the Son of Man and drink his blood, you have no life in you." (John 6:53) Christ is perfectly clear. We are made God's children in Baptism, and nourished and sustained in the faith by the Word and the Lord's Supper. That's how we come to believe in Jesus in the first place, and how we persevere until the end. People apprehend this through faith. And this Baptism and faith are completed in the resurrection (Romans 6:5).

To drive home the point about Baptism, you can also direct the hearer's attention to the pall and how it signifies the robe of Christ's righteousness that the blessed departed received in Baptism, which covered all of his sin. You can speak to the name of the Holy Trinity and the sign of the cross that was placed upon him at his Baptism, at the commendation, and will be done finally at the committal before his body is laid to rest. You can speak to the blessed departed's faith in all that Baptism promises, and how he received the means of grace which kept him in the true faith unto life everlasting. You can invite the hearers to have the same faith.

You can also overtly use the funeral sermon as an opportunity to invite the hearers to come to church. If they are from the area, invite them to the church you serve in particular. Tell them you would be happy to find them a faithful church in their area. Be bold so that they might find comfort in the means of grace and Christian encouragement in the communion of saints (cf. Hebrews 10:25).

You need to state the benefits of the means of grace. Repentance and faith in the Word of Jesus matter. As best as you are able, say things in such a way that the hearer cannot fit a false idea into your words. Otherwise, the hearers could be distracted from Christ, if they think that everyone for whom they have affection goes to heaven, making Jesus superfluous instead of the only way to the Father.

5.

"Speak Well of Them" (But Not Too Much)

Is the sermon only about Christ
or about the blessed departed's life in Christ?

D O NOT DO EULOGIES. They conflict with the comfort of Christ that you seek to impart. There is a time and a place to talk about memories, but the funeral is not the place to dwell on them. To do so would be to supplant the purpose of the funeral by looking backwards only to memories and the life that was lived, instead of forward to the life that still lives in soul and will live forever in body and soul in the resurrection. Many a "Celebration of Life" has erred in this regard.

Still, funeral sermons need not be so generic that they could be preached at any Christian's funeral. In the *Small Catechism*, Luther reminds us that we are to "speak well" of our neighbor. This is solid counsel for funeral sermons, too. No, we do not do eulogies, but there is a temptation to overreact to eulogies and say nothing about the blessed departed. This is a mistake. Funerals are not just about Jesus, but about Jesus *and* His life with this child of God.

Speak, therefore, about the life of Christ through this particular individual. Remember to thank God for the good that the departed "was permitted to give and receive."[5] The deceased individual has a name to which God has attached His name in Holy Baptism. So, to disregard his name is to overlook this marvelous truth. This individual Christian was brought into Christ's Body as one of His beloved members. True, "He must increase, but I must decrease," as John the Baptist said (John 3:30), but that hardly means the blessed departed disappears any more than John did.

---

[5] *Lutheran Service Book: Agenda*, 110.

You can and should talk about the fruit of faith in Christ. Being careful not to give the impression that this fruit saved anyone, you can proclaim how God worked through the blessed departed in the church, in his family, among friends, and so on. You can speak about the blessed departed's confession of sin, reception of the means of grace, confession of the Creed, and good works that flowed from his faith in Christ. Scripture does this: "'Blessed are the dead who die in the Lord from now on.' 'Blessed indeed,' says the Spirit, 'that they may rest from their labors, for their deeds follow them!'" (Revelation 14:13)

Some pastors keep a journal on particular members throughout their tenure at a congregation. This helps them keep in mind the time they spent with their members so that when a member dies, they can give specific examples of the faithful Christian life he lived. Even if you are not so organized, though, you can think upon bedside visits, if applicable, or other times where the Christian confession came out.

A few examples of this will help. A member was in his last days and could not talk or eat. He could move his head and arms, though. As I was finishing a devotion, he motioned his hand toward his mouth. His wife said, "He wants the Lord's Supper." He then nodded his head in agreement. I mentioned this in my sermon for his funeral. Another example is a member with Alzheimer's who would sing hymns and the liturgy with me. I mentioned this in my sermon for her funeral (and have more members with Alzheimer's for whom this will apply in the future). One more example bears mentioning. When a current member's wife was in her last days, and I was visiting her more often, he was struck by the Third Article of the Creed. As we all partook of Holy Communion, he remarked how comforting it was that his wife was receiving the forgiveness of sins in faith because it leads to "the resurrection of the body, and the life everlasting." If I am privileged to do this member's funeral, I will include this faithful confession in my sermon. These types of moments are gems that prove the point: you can speak well of these dear Christians while exalting Christ's work for them, upon them, and through them. Their faithfulness to the end was shown most in their eagerness to hear the Gospel and receive the Lord's body and blood for their forgiveness, life, and salvation.

Without making it all about them, speak well of them. As best as you are able, say things in such a way that the hearer cannot fit a false idea into your words. You certainly do not want to distract from Christ, but Christ did not come just in some general sense. He came for individuals, including the one for whose funeral you are preaching.

6.

Let Them Cry,
But Give Them Hope

*Must we be only happy, or are we allowed
to weep over death like Jesus did?*

A MEMBER DIED, and her son told me that he was happy about it. He said that she was in heaven, so why should he be sad? It was as if he believed that weeping would have been a sign of unbelief. This is more common an idea than I had originally realized. A former member of the congregation I serve, no matter how many times I corrected him, would haughtily judge those who wept at funerals as if it were a sign of their unbelief. Then there are those I have heard on their death bed say to their family, "I am going to be in a better place, so be happy." While some people have every good intention when they say such things, it is not the way Scripture teaches us. No, we do not want utter despair in the heart of anyone. One can, however, weep with faith.

Take Jesus as the prime example. "Jesus wept." (John 11:35) This showed that He loved Lazarus. "See how He loved him!" they said (John 11:36). Jesus wept even knowing that He was going to raise Lazarus from the dead. He wept because He knew more than anyone that death is our enemy. That we were never supposed to die. That death is the end of a temporal future and separation in this life from those you love. Sorrow proves love. It is why a wife might get weepy when her parents leave to go home far away after a short visit. Moreover, faithful Christian sorrow is a good work, because Jesus did it. Jesus was "A man of sorrows and acquainted with grief" (Isaiah 53:3), and He wept for the right reasons.

So let your members cry. Let them weep because, though they know death is the last enemy to be destroyed (1 Corinthians 15:26), it still brings sorrow to their sanctified hearts. We are happy that our believing loved one is in heaven, but are still given to weep over death like Jesus did.

Our tears, however, are mixed with joy. Give them hope, too:

> But we do not want you to be uninformed, brothers, about those who are asleep, that you may not grieve as others do who have no hope. For since we believe that Jesus died and rose again, even so, through Jesus, God will bring with him those who have fallen asleep. (1 Thessalonians 4:13–14)

Luther used these verses more than any other to comfort Christians at the time of death. He taught that while we have grief, it is mixed with the hope that Jesus' death and resurrection give. You can let the mourners know their loved one is still with Christ and has the life of their risen Lord. For the Christian, death is not just an enemy but also a defeated enemy. It is now a source of hope for Christians for their own resurrection because Christ has "the keys of death." (Revelation 1:18) This is why our hymns proclaim beautiful truths like this:

> Jesus lives! And now is death
> But the gate of life immortal;
> This shall calm my trembling breath
> When I pass its gloomy portal.
> Faith shall cry, as fails each sense:
> Jesus is my confidence![6]

It should be noted that those who are mourning will inevitably try to get rid of their sorrow some other way. They will say that others have it worse than they do. They will try to drown the tears with pleasurable times. They will attempt to work it away by keeping busy and being industrious. But these will not cure sorrow. Hope in Christ is the only true cure of sorrow. Give them that certain hope that Christ's death and resurrection alone bring, so that their faith is firmly grounded.

So let them cry, but give them hope. As best as you are able, say things in such a way that the hearer cannot fit a false idea into your words. Otherwise, your hearers could be distracted from Christ, because they do not see death as an enemy worth grieving and therefore do not long for the resurrection of the body, which stems from the firstfruits of Christ's own resurrection (1 Corinthians 15:20).

---

[6] LSB 490, 5; TLH 201, 5.

7.

The Goal of the Resurrection of the Body

Is heaven good enough, or do you also
"look for the resurrection of the dead"?

PREACH HEAVEN. The soul of the faithful departed is there with Christ. Saint Paul wrote that he would "rather be away from the body and at home with the Lord" (2 Corinthians 5:8). Again he wrote,

> To live is Christ and to die is gain ... I am hard pressed between the two. My desire is to depart and be with Christ, for that is far better. But to remain in the flesh is more necessary on your account (Philippians 1:21, 23–24).

Jesus also told the account of the rich man and Lazarus, where the angels ushered Lazarus to Abraham's bosom (Luke 16:22). So by all means, proclaim heaven as the intermediary state of the soul for those who died with faith in Christ. Any Roman Catholics at the funeral may assume purgatory is the intermediary state instead, where the souls of those who died in God's grace and friendship need to achieve the holiness or purification needed before they can finally arrive in the joys of a pain-free heaven. We need to condemn this synergistic way to thinking, and affirm the joy of heaven immediately for those who have died trusting in our Lord Jesus and His righteousness for salvation.

Too many people, moreover, wrongly think the pre-resurrection heaven is our permanent home. They think that all we have to look forward to after death is becoming spirits in the sky. This lends toward the popular myth that we become angels when we die, and not just "like" the angels, as Jesus actually said (Matthew 22:30). Many people think heaven is the end, and we become bodiless spirits forever. I remember a seminary classmate who once preached in class that the body is just a shell, prompting another class-mate to point out the inherent Gnosticism in such a proclamation.

Heaven, however, is not the end. Death is not the end of your bodily existence. The resurrection is the continuation of it. Christ died and rose bodily to life again. With the Head come His members: "And God raised the Lord and will also raise us up by his power." (1 Corinthians 6:14) Saint Paul wrote, "The last enemy to be defeated is death." (1 Corinthians 15:26) Saint John wrote about the souls of those slain for the word of God, asking, "How long before you will judge and avenge our blood on those who dwell on the earth?" (Revelation 6:10). Saint Paul also wrote the words which include what you speak at the graveside during the committal:

> But our citizenship is in heaven, and from it we await a Savior, the Lord Jesus Christ, who will transform our lowly body to be like his glorious body, by the power that enables him even to subject all things to himself. (Philippians 3:20–21)

Heaven, therefore, is certainly something to speak about, since our citizenship is there, but we also await the day when our Lord Jesus transforms these mortal bodies and clothes His saints in immortality (cf. 1 Corinthians 15:53–56). Like Job, we know that our Redeemer lives, and on the Last Day we will behold Him standing upon this earth. Even though our skin is destroyed, yet in our flesh we shall see God (Job 19:25–27), and He "will swallow up death forever" (Isaiah 25:8).

This truth is a great place to connect the means of grace in your preaching, as well. Saint Paul wrote that we are baptized into Christ's death and resurrection, and he concludes, "For if we have been united with him in a death like his, we shall certainly be united with him in a resurrection like his." (Romans 6:5) Jesus also promised, "Whoever feeds on my flesh and drinks my blood has eternal life, and I will raise him up on the last day." (John 6:54) Jesus also promised, "I am the resurrection and the life. Whoever believes in me, though he die, yet shall he live, and everyone who lives and believes in me shall never die." (John 11:25–26) These last verses are a reminder that while all will be resurrected, only those who trust in Jesus will be resurrected to eternal life, a point to keep in mind while preaching this blessed truth (cf. John 5:28–29).

The Church's faith in the resurrection is also why we say, "Rest in Peace." Jesus tells His disciples, "Our friend Lazarus has fallen asleep, but I go to awaken him" (John 11:11), just like He says Jairus' daughter is "sleeping" before He raises her (Matthew 9:24). The dead in Christ are alive in their souls, but sleeping in their bodies and awaiting their awakening at the resurrection (cf. Daniel 12:2). This is a comforting truth to confess, especially in the age of cremation. When I put my kids to bed and wish them a good night's sleep, I do not then proceed to start them on fire! They go to sleep, and I expect them to wake up again! In the exact same way, we expect our Lord to awaken the bodies of "those who are asleep" in Him (1 Thessalonians 4:13). So we sing in the hymn:

> Teach me to live that I may dread
> The grave as little as my bed.
> Teach me to die that so I may
> Rise glorious at the awe-full Day.[7]

Articulate both heaven and the resurrection. As best as you are able, say things in such a way that the hearer cannot fit a false idea into your words. Otherwise, your hearers could be distracted from the fullness of Christ's promise of eternal life, because they would not "look for the resurrection of the dead and the life of the world to come." The last stanza of "Lord, Thee I Love with All My Heart," helps you articulate both truths:

> Lord, let at last Thine angels come,
> To Abr'ham's bosom bear me home,
> That I may die unfearing;
> And in its narrow chamber keep
> My body safe in peaceful sleep
> Until Thy reappearing.
> And then from death awaken me
> That these mine eyes with joy may see,
> O Son of God, Thy glorious face,
> My Savior and my fount of grace.
> Lord Jesus Christ, my prayer attend, my prayer attend,
> And I will praise Thee without end.[8]

---

[7] LSB 883, 3; TLH 558, 3. Besides "sleep," see all of the *mortis dulcia nomia* (sweet names of death) in Francis Pieper, *Christian Dogmatics: Vol. 3* (St. Louis: Concordia Publishing House, 1968), 511.

[8] LSB 708, 3; TLH 429, 3.

8.

The Last Confession
of the Dead in Christ

Is the funeral only for the living, or also for the dead?

YOU WILL HEAR PEOPLE SAY that the funeral is for the living and not the dead. It sounds pious, as if they just mean that their loved one is in heaven and so what really matters is comforting those living. There is often, however, something more sinister going on with that statement. Sometimes they are really saying that the focus of the funeral should not be on Christ and the blessed departed's faith in Christ but on *them*, the living. Which means they get to determine what is important about the funeral. They get to use the funeral as an occasion for things they like: their preferred music, their favorite hymns or songs, or eulogies that they come up with, which are almost always frivolous Christ-less fluff, often overly emotional sentimentality, or occasionally even outright heresy. That is hardly a pious intent!

Pastors can also get caught up in the idea that the funeral is for the living. They do this often in order to justify preaching at funerals for those who have no connection to their church, or any other Christian church, for that matter. "It's an opportunity to share the Gospel to those still living," they might say. "How can I pass that up? The funeral is for the living, after all, not the dead." So, they preach around the dead's lack of a life with Christ in His means of grace and just proclaim a generic Gospel to those living. For this, it should be noted, they collect an honorarium and the praise of men. All in the name of the funeral being for the living, not the dead.

The funeral is not just for the living. It is also for the dead in Christ to proclaim the true faith to those they leave behind. It is for the blessed departed to confess one last time that he was a Christian here on earth, and remains one in heaven until the resurrection. It is for him to confess how he clings to Jesus' cross and resurrection. That the means of grace were the instruments by which the Holy Spirit engendered and nourished his faith in Christ. That he is presently in heaven because of this and longs for the resurrection of the body and the life everlasting in the new creation. That he confessed his faith and lived it out in various ways in his earthly life. The funeral is for the living to hear the confession of the dead in Christ, whose soul is living with his Savior in heaven. The funeral is not taking place because of the living. It is happening because of the dead. So, you preach what the dead believed and what he wants those present to believe.

An example of this is a grandmother who told me before she died that she prays for her grandchildren because she wants them to be Christians. Mentioning this in the sermon was a way to speak directly to those grandchildren in the stead of their grandma. Another example is mentioning how the dead in Christ wanted his body treated with care, giving it the dignity that his Baptism and the resurrection demand. The dead in Christ can definitely keep confessing through their funeral.

So, as best as you are able, say things in such a way that the hearer cannot fit a false idea into your words. Your hearers could get distracted from Christ by a funeral focused on the desires of the living instead of the Christian confession of the one who died in Christ.

SERMON 1.

"Jesus Knows Shirley"

(JOHN 10:27–30)

Dear family of Shirley, dear friends, dear brothers and sisters in Christ:

Grace, mercy, and peace to you from God our Father
and our Lord Jesus Christ. **Amen.**

Y<small>OU ALL KNOW</small> S<small>HIRLEY</small> in your own way. But here in this service, we will not be dwelling so much on how *you* know Shirley. Don't get me wrong, there is a time and a place for that. For the stories about how hard working she was at home and on the farm. For recounting how much she enjoyed gardening and how she gave loving attention to each of her children and grandchildren. For the happy memories like when she, one Easter, gave her kids Snap, Crackle, and Pop (a story I just recently heard about), three little lambs for her three dear children. Reminiscing surely has its place, and you have been, and will continue to do so as family and friends. Good. Thanks be to God for the love she was allowed to give and to receive. But *now*, in *this service*, we are here not to talk about all the ways that *you* know Shirley, but all the ways that *Jesus* does.

Jesus tells us, "My sheep hear my voice, and I *know* them." So, *Jesus* knows Shirley. But how? It is one thing to know Shirley as a mother or a grandmother or a friend, or even, as for me, as a parishioner. But it is an entirely different and *wonderful* thing for *Jesus* to know her. So, let's focus our attention on that blessed reality. On how *Jesus* knows Shirley better than all of us.

You see, Jesus knew Shirley before she was even born. Not just because He is the eternal Son of God who knows everything before it happens. But because, before time began, Jesus *chose* her to be His sheep. We call this eternal election. It is a comforting mystery that God has revealed to us in the Bible. Jesus elected Shirley; He knew her even before creation in the sense that He selected her to be His own sheep. Which means that no one could snatch her out of His hand. That no one could snatch her out of His Father's hand. That He and His Father are one in essence and in will, and God's will was to save Shirley eternally.

Which brings us to another way that Jesus *knows* Shirley. He knows her sins. Again, not just because He is the eternal Son of God who knows everything. Yes, He did know her sin in that way too. He knows *all of the world's* sin in that way. The *original* sin that we have all inherited from the first sinner, Adam, which left us all without fear, love, and trust in God. Those *actual* sins of thought, word, and deed. Jesus knows it all. And He also knows that the wages of our sin is death. He knows that this is why Shirley died: because of her sin. He knows that this is why *you* are going to die, too. But that's not what I mean by saying that Jesus knows her sins…

Rather, Jesus knows her sins *because He bore her sins in His own body and paid for them.* That's how Jesus knows Shirley's sins! God counted *her* sins against *Him* on the cross. Jesus in love laid down His life for Shirley as her Good Shepherd. He died her death for her. He gave His perfect life in her place upon the cross, suffering her penalty for her every sin, burying them in the grave, and rising victorious over sin, death, and the devil *for her. This* is how Jesus knows Shirley's sins. By remembering them no more. By forgiving them. By washing them away by His blood.

Which brings us to yet another way that Jesus *knows* Shirley: through His Word and His Sacraments. Jesus *gained* her salvation on the cross and in His resurrection from the dead. But He *gave* her salvation through His Word and Sacraments.

He *baptized* her with water and the Spirit, giving her faith in Him and making her as pure in His sight as a white wooled little lamb.

And as Shirley grew up, Jesus spoke His comforting Word to her, and she listened to Him like sheep listen to their shepherd. "My sheep hear my voice," Jesus says. That's how *Jesus* knew *Shirley* and how *Shirley* knew *Jesus.* Shirley heard Jesus' voice in His Word and Sacrament and she trusted in Him. She followed Him. And this kept her safe from the danger of the devil, this world, and her own sinful flesh.

Shirley came to church and was a lifelong member here at Trinity, hearing Jesus' voice throughout her life. I myself was privileged to have known her for ten years now and remember seeing her sitting right over there in that pew listening to Jesus' Word of forgiveness, life, and salvation; watching her come to this altar feeding upon the life-giving body and blood of Jesus; visiting her in Bill and Deb's home when she couldn't make it to church but church came to her to let her know she is still part of the flock; and for the last few years over at the Lutheran Home, she heard her Good Shepherd's voice too.

Just last week, in fact, in her room there, I heard her confess her sins after which she heard the voice of Jesus say, "I forgive you" one last time. Just last week I heard her join in with her frail voice as we prayed to "Our Father who art in heaven" together. Just last week I watched her move her arms in delight when I would sing of her Savior Jesus to her and the life He won for her. Yes, Shirley heard the voice of her Good Shepherd by listening to and trusting in His life-giving promises until the day the angels brought her soul to Jesus in heaven.

And so, Jesus *knows* her in *that* way too. As He said about His sheep, "I *give* them eternal life, and they will never perish." Jesus *gave* Shirley eternal life just as He promised. Yes, her *body* is now lifeless here and will be laid to rest in peace. But her *soul* has the eternal life Jesus promised her. He now knows her in heaven. He has folded His sheep to His breast and Shirley lays in His arms to rest, as we just sang.

But even *that* beautiful reality is not the end of how Jesus knows Shirley. What's more, when the trumpet blasts and the Lord finally comes back, He will raise Shirley's *body* and reunite it to her *soul*. In an instant, He will turn her mortal body into an immortal one. Her perishable body into an imperishable. He will not let *any part of her* perish but will give her eternal life *body* and soul in a new creation. And *then* Jesus will know Shirley forever in Paradise, bringing to completion what He planned for her before the foundation of this world.

So, *this* is how Jesus knows Shirley. And He knows *all who hear His voice* in the same way. Not all *will* end up in heaven. Not all *will* rejoice in the resurrection. *Only* those who hear the voice of the Good Shepherd in faith like Shirley did will. So, hear His voice in faith yourselves. Rejoice in how He knows *your* sin too. Again, not just because He knows all things, but because He took all your sin upon Himself on the cross, laying down His life *for you too*. Delight in His forgiving and life-giving Word and Sacrament like Shirley did by going to a faithful church and trusting that you are a sheep of the Good Shepherd like she is. Receive the eternal life He gives as a free gift. And not only will Jesus know you like He knows Shirley. Not only will you know Jesus like Shirley knows Him. But you will know *Shirley* forever, as well. Not just reminiscing about the good old times that happened long ago. But rejoicing eternally in the resurrection with her and Jesus and Ray and all believers who have gone before us and will come after us.

This is why, as much as we love talking about how *you* know Shirley, we take the time to focus on how *Jesus* knows her. Because though Shirley has left a lasting memory, *Jesus* has left an *everlasting* one. So, rejoice with all the sheep of the Good Shepherd, even as you mourn. Jesus knows His sheep, including Shirley. They will never perish. And no one will snatch them out of His hand.

In Jesus' Name. **Amen.**

SERMON 2.

"Meeting the Lord in the Air with Don"

(1 THESSALONIANS 4:13–18)

Dear family of Don, especially you, Jocille, dear friends,
dear brothers and sisters in Christ:

Grace, mercy, and peace to you from God our Father
and our Lord Jesus Christ. **Amen.**

WE WILL *MEET THE LORD IN THE AIR*. That's the promise Scripture gives to all who trust in our Lord Jesus Christ. When that Last Day comes and the Lord Himself descends from heaven "with a cry of command, with the voice of an archangel, and with the sound of the trumpet of God," all those who in this life clung to Jesus by faith will *"meet the Lord in the air…"* The dead in Christ will rise first, including Don, whose *soul* is currently in heaven but whose *body* we will lay to rest in peace today until that *Great* Day. And then, immediately after the dead in Christ rise, those who are alive until the Lord's coming, "will be caught up together with them in the clouds to *meet the Lord in the air…"* That's God's certain promise to all who cling to Christ.

And to *meet the Lord in the air* is especially appropriate for *Don*. Don spent no small amount of time in the air as a Navy pilot. Don spent no small amount of time looking *into* the air as an Air Traffic Controller, too. Don enjoyed the *fresh* air while gardening and fishing, looking up into the air while hunting pheasants, and on the hobby farm, gazing up into the *air* at the apples hanging from the trees. *And* Don's soul flew *through* the air on the wings of the angels last Saturday morning, when the Lord sent those ministering spirits to harvest Don's *soul* to heaven until the great harvest of our *bodies* on the day of the resurrection, when Don's body and soul will

24

be reunited, glorified forever. So, what a fitting truth to ponder when it comes to Don. Don will *meet the Lord in the air*.

And so will all of you who live in repentance and faith in Jesus. This is how one gets to heaven and to the resurrection where we *meet the Lord in the air*: through repentance and faith.

Don knew this well. Though he forgot so much at the end of his life, the Lord let Don remember this. He let Don remember that he was a sinner. A sinner who could not earn his way to heaven by any number of good works. A sinner who deserved death as the wages of his sin, and hell too. That's what you deserve, and what I deserve, as well. And without repentance and faith in Jesus, that's what each of us would get. It's what many *do* get because of their refusal to repent and believe. *But* it is *not* what Don got. No, Don repented of his sin and trusted in Jesus Christ as his Savior. Again, his soul flew through the *air* on the wings of the angels to heaven last week.

And I know this because I was privileged to minister to Don at the end of his life. When I first met him a couple of years ago, he remembered a bit more. I'll never forget telling him that his teacher in the one room schoolhouse he attended as a boy was also a member of our congregation, Miss Miller—now Mrs. Belfield, a shut-in still living in Cedar Rapids. She had told me a story about Don when she found out he and you, Jocille, had joined our congregation. How one day a war plane flew over the schoolhouse and Don and the other kids went outside to watch it zoom overhead *in the air*. No doubt that had just a *little* influence on his future! That was a couple of years ago now, and at that point Don remembered.

But I was privileged to minister to Don not just when he remembered the memories of the past. I was also privileged to minister to Don when he remembered precious little. And spoke precious little. But what he did remember was *precious*. And what he did remember is what saved him, and what made it such a privilege to minister to him. Don remembered the One Who remembered him. Don remembered Jesus. Don trusted in Him, who said, "I, when I am lifted up from the earth, will draw all people to Myself" (John 12:32). Jesus drew Don to Himself. Lifted up *in the air* on the cross, dying for Don's sins, Jesus drew Don to Himself. Don met *the Lord in the air* many times as he recalled how Jesus was lifted up *into the air* on the cross *for him*. Don not only repented of his sin but *what's more*, he firmly trusted that all his guilt Jesus took upon Himself on the cross. All his punishment Jesus paid. All that was needed for Don's salvation God's Son made flesh accomplished *for him*. Completely. "It is finished," Jesus cried out in the *air* on the cross. And God the Father added His "Amen! Your salvation *is* accomplished!" when He raised His Son from the dead in the cool *air* of the garden on Easter morning. Don believed that. Don remembered that. And if there is one thing worth remembering even if you were to forget all else, it is that precious truth of God's grace in the cross and resurrection of Jesus Christ, our Savior.

Now, obviously, Don was not there when they crucified our Lord. But we know what Jesus means when He says He draws all people, including Don, to Himself. He means that He proclaims His Gospel to them, that Good News of what He has done, so that they trust in Him. And Don heard that Gospel, that Good News of Jesus Christ, *and Don trusted in Him.* Don *was* there as I proclaimed the cross of Christ to him these last two years at the Lutheran Home. Don *was* there as I reminded him that he was baptized into Jesus' death and resurrection, and that whoever believes and is baptized shall be saved. Don *was* there as I pronounced the Absolution that releases sinners from their bondage to sin. Don *was* there as I distributed to him the body and blood of his Savior, Jesus, which gave him pardon and peace with God and a foretaste of the feast that is to come.

And not only was Don there, he received all of this *in faith*, trusting that he, a sinner, was saved entirely by God's grace alone in Christ Jesus, his Savior. And Don received this not just *from me* these last two years but from other faithful ministers of the Word and throughout his adult life. Don trusted in the Gospel of Jesus Christ which he regularly received. And this faith alone saved him. This faith alone in Christ alone is why Don not only dwells *now* with his *soul* in heaven, but will also *meet the Lord in the air* with his glorified *body* on the Day of the Resurrection.

And I pray the same for each and every one of you. Repentance and faith in Jesus Christ are how *you too* will get to heaven and to that glorious day of *meeting the Lord in the air. Don* knew this well. Know it well *yourselves.* There is nothing more freeing than to confess your sins and to be drawn to Jesus, lifted up *in the air* on the cross. To gaze at Him dying for your every sin. To look at Him taking your death upon Himself. To see Him suffer hell itself and be forsaken by God so that God will never forsake you. Never. No, He loves you dearly. Each and every one of you. How could He not; He gave His only Son into death for your sins! This is what Don believed as he received the Gospel of Jesus Christ until his dying day. And it saved him. Continue to hear the same Gospel and believe it yourselves. And it will save you, too.

And it will also help you as you grieve Don's death. We Christians do not grieve as others do who have no hope. We grieve, yes, as we share memories of Don; we weep, we miss him, we wish he was here. As we should; Jesus wept too. Our sorrow is evidence that we love Don. *But* we also have hope. Certain hope. Because just as Jesus died and rose again, so too He will bring with Him those who have fallen asleep, even Don. Jesus is the resurrection and the life, as He said. So, keep Jesus lifted up *in the air* on the cross before yourselves. Keep Jesus lifted from His grave to the *fresh air* of the garden in your hearts. And the Lord is with you. And He will guide you to that Day when we all *meet the Lord in the air* with Don. So that we will always be with the Lord.

In Jesus' Name. **Amen.**

SERMON 3.

"Kenneth Believed This"

(John 11:17–27)

Alleluia! Christ is risen! **He is risen, indeed! Alleluia!**

Dear family of Kenneth, especially you Rosemaree, dear friends and family of God:

"DO YOU BELIEVE THIS?" Jesus asked Martha this essential question after telling her, "I am the resurrection and the life. Whoever believes in me, though he die, yet shall he live, and everyone who lives and believes in me shall never die." The context is important. Martha's brother Lazarus had just died. He was a young man, whose life was stolen in its prime. He was a dear friend of Jesus, as were his two sisters, Mary and Martha. And Jesus asked Martha this essential question, "Do you believe this?" in regard to whether she believed He had power over death itself.

"Do you believe this?" Kenneth did. I used to ask this same question to him and to you, Rosemaree, after reciting to you both the Confession of sin during my monthly calls at your place. You and Kenneth would say, "Yes," and you would receive the Absolution, the forgiveness of sins that Jesus purchased by His death on the cross and which guarantees eternal life to all who trust in it. Yes, Kenneth was—and *remains*—a Christian. Which means that while on earth he believed that he was a sinner. That he had earned the wages of death for his sin. That he should confess that sin. And in confessing it, he had great comfort in the forgiveness that Jesus gave to him, full and free, that gave him life eternal. I heard from Kenneth's own mouth more times than I can count that he believed this.

"Do you believe this?" Kenneth did. There is no doubt in my mind about it. Even throughout COVID, until just the last couple of months, Kenneth was here in church on Sunday morning. Not only did he have me come by monthly to see you, Rosemaree, but he made sure he was here in church each week, as well. He had promised he *would* be when he was confirmed.

And he was a man of honesty and integrity. He held the confession of the truth of Jesus Christ precious. If you viewed his body, yesterday, you saw his Small Catechism beside him. The Small Catechism is a simple explanation of Christianity that we use in the Lutheran Church as a handbook and prayerbook of the Christian faith. Kenneth believed this, too, and his life showed it.

"Do you believe this?" Kenneth did. The *other* book you might have seen just above Kenneth's body was The Lutheran Hymnal. When Kenneth was learning the Small Catechism as a boy, his pastor would sing with him and all the others in his confirmation class. Kenneth and I used to talk about those good ol' days all the time. He and I both love to sing. And I will miss singing the Doxology with him *here below*, though I know that he is singing praise *above* with all the heavenly host to Father, Son, and Holy Ghost just as we did here on earth. The Lutheran Church has long been known as the "singing church" because our services involve so much of it. We believe that we sing the faith, confessing what we believe in song. And Kenneth believed this, too.

"Do you believe this?" Kenneth did. He believed God's Word. He believed every word of it. He was a Christian—and *remains* one. Kenneth's *body* is merely sleeping like the body of Lazarus was. But his *soul* lives in heaven. Kenneth rejoices with the angels. After a long life—94½ years—Jesus finally sent His angels to bring Kenneth into His nearer presence. With all those who believed in Jesus from years past, including his son Ricky, who like Lazarus lost his life far too soon, who like Lazarus has two sisters here, and who, like Lazarus depended on Jesus for life and resurrection. Kenneth believed he would see Ricky again because of this promise of Jesus. Yes, Kenneth believed this Word of God, and now he sees his son, and the eternal Son of the Father in heaven, and awaits the great day of resurrection. Yes, Kenneth believed it, and so he is blessed forever.

"Do you believe this?" Martha did. Her response to Jesus is so beautiful. "Yes, Lord; I believe that you are the Christ, the Son of God, who is coming into the world." She trusted that Jesus is the Son of God made flesh who came into the world to save her and *all* the world. And He did. He died for the world. He paid the penalty for the guilt of our sin, every one of us. And all who repent of their sin and believe in Him, *benefit* from what He has done, and seek to abide in His Word unto the end. But Jesus was not just asking Martha about her faith in *that*. More particularly, He was asking her if she believed that He could raise her brother Lazarus from the dead. And she said, "Yes, Lord." And then Jesus *did*! *That* part I did not read, but Saint John's Gospel goes on and tells us that Jesus went to the tomb and said, "Lazarus, come out!" And Lazarus walked out of the tomb *alive* to rejoin his two sisters and all who loved him here on earth.

"Do you believe this?" You might want to say, "Well, I believe it, but I want Jesus to do that for *me*, too." No doubt Kenneth and you, Rosemaree, wanted that when it came to Ricky. To receive him back in *this* life. And no doubt we'd like to have *Kenneth* back in *this* life, too. His family knows more than any how great of a man he was to have around and how much he will be missed. He was kind. He was thoughtful. He was funny. He was a man of character. He was a faithful and loving husband. A gracious and attentive father. A grandfather any would covet to have. To me and my family, he showed much love and attention, and I can only imagine how much more so he gave to his own blood. He razzed me for owning anything but a Ford, especially when my Chevy broke down outside his apartment—thanks again Lee for the jump. He always had a story about fishing or playing cards or his confirmation class or the way the Germans were treated during the World Wars and how Williams was originally Wilhelm until those hard days. Yes, and if *I* will miss Kenneth, which I will very much, I can only imagine how much his family and friends will miss him even more, and, at times, wish that he were back here with us, raised like Lazarus.

But here's the thing: one day *he will be*. That's the whole point, the goal of the Christian religion. We believe in the resurrection of the body and the life everlasting. We believe that *Jesus* is the Resurrection and the Life. We believe that He is God's Son who came into the world to save sinners. We believe that He fulfilled God's Law for us, that He died for our sin and rose triumphantly, so that we have victory over sin, death, and the devil in Him. We believe that all who are baptized into Christ's death and resurrection and trust in Him are righteous in God's sight and really are saved forever. I believe this. Kenneth believed this. "Do *you* believe this?"

Believe it, and you will see Kenneth again. Believe it and you will see him with Ricky, with Lazarus and Martha and their sister Mary. Believe it, and *with* all those who believed in Jesus in times past, who believe in Him in the present, and who will believe in Him into the future, you will experience one day the resurrection to eternal life. Not all will. Some will be raised to eternal destruction. But Jesus does not want that for you. That is why He died for you. That is why He offers in His Church the forgiveness of sins and the promise of life everlasting, and why Kenneth found such comfort in the Christian Church and the communion of saints. Kenneth believed that Jesus did this all for *him*. And He did it for *you*, too. So, "Do *you* believe this?" Believe it, and you will have not just days with Kenneth that you can look *back* on fondly. Believe it, and you will have days with him that you can look *forward* to, as well. Believe with Martha, with Kenneth, with the whole Christian Church, that Easter is real. That Christ is risen. That His life gives Kenneth life and all of us life. Say with Martha, "Yes, Lord, I believe that you have power over death itself," and your tears will be mixed with joy that you will see Kenneth again in resurrected glory with all who trust in our living Savior, Jesus Christ.

Alleluia! Christ is risen! **He is risen, indeed! Alleluia!**

SERMON 4.

"The Lord's Power Made Perfect in Nathan's Weakness"

(2 Corinthians 12:7–10)

Dear family of Nathan, especially you Ashley, Lily, and Noah, dear friends,
dear brothers and sisters in Christ:

Grace, mercy, and peace to you from God our Father
and our Lord Jesus Christ. **Amen.**

NATHAN BOASTED IN HIS WEAKNESS like St. Paul did. Diagnosed before becoming a teenager with Loeys-Dietz Syndrome, Nathan knew that the Lord's power is made perfect in weakness. In Nathan's words, "If me having Loeys-Dietz Syndrome brings people to Christ, then I'm happy to be used in this way." Nathan's weakness *did* bring people to speak to him about his syndrome, providing him many opportunities to give the reason for the hope that was within him: namely, God's grace in Jesus Christ, his Savior. So, Nathan boasted in his weakness.

And, now that Nathan has died due to this syndrome, death being the ultimate weakness, *Nathan can still boast. Even in the weakness of death.* Not only because Nathan's soul lives in heaven and his body will be raised to glory, something we will consider in a moment. But also, because Nathan's death has brought all of you here. And so, it provides me opportunity to speak to all of you on behalf of Nathan about the hope he had in Jesus. So that *you too* might have the same hope in our Redeemer. So that *you too* might boast in your weaknesses, believing with Nathan that our Lord's grace is sufficient for you; for His power is made perfect in weakness.

Nathan's hope in Jesus began with his knowledge of his central weakness. Nathan believed he was a sinner. All people are. But Nathan truly believed it. He knew that sin is a condition just as real as Loeys-Dietz, and even more deadly. Sin is why death has come into this world and why everyone dies, whatever the secondary causes may be. The wages of sin is death. *But*, the gift of God is eternal life in Christ Jesus our Lord (Rom. 6:23). And Nathan believed this all the more! He believed what Scripture says of him and Jesus: "For while we were still *weak*, at the right time Christ died for the ungodly" (Rom. 5:6). So, Nathan boasted in this weakness. Not that he boasted in his sin. No, Nathan repented of that. As his pastor, I heard him confess his sin more times than I can count, even over Zoom calls these last two months. No, Nathan boasted in his weak condition of being a sinner *because he believed that Jesus came for sinners.*

This was Nathan's hope *and what Nathan wants you all to believe too.* Jesus came for you. Because you too are weak sinners in need of a Savior. And Jesus Christ is *your* Savior, as well. In His grace, His undeserved love, God saw you in your lost condition, in your sin, and chose to save you. He sent His Son down to earth to become a man, yet without sin. To live a perfect life on your behalf under God's Law. And in the *weakness* of the cross, God condemned all of your sin in His Son, Jesus. In the *weakness* of the cross, God accepted Jesus' perfect life as a substitute for your sinful ones. His power was made perfect in *weakness* as He died on that cross to save you. And He showed forth that power three days later when He rose from the grave, the victor over sin, death and hell for Nathan, for you, and for all sinners in the world. Jesus now offers you His victory for free, the forgiveness of sins and the gift of eternal life.

Nathan would have you hear this Gospel, this Good News of Jesus Christ, today because it is the power of God for salvation for all who believe (Rom. 1:16). Nathan believed it. I know he did because I heard him confess Christ as his Savior, again, more times than I can count, bringing his wife and children to church faithfully so that they too would know Christ and His love. And most recently, Nathan confessed Christ from his hospital bed in Boston, as Ashley can attest, showing forth his faith in Jesus as he moved his mouth while we sang "Praise God from whom all blessings flow." And as he put his fingers to his mouth asking for the Lord's Supper, the Bread of Life that strengthened and preserved him so many years unto life everlasting. Yes, Nathan believed this Good News of Jesus Christ throughout his life and to the very end. *And Nathan would have you believe it yourselves.* Jesus says, "I am the way, and the truth, and the life. No one comes to the Father except through me" (Jn 14:6). Without faith in this, you do not benefit from it. But with faith, you do! So, trust that Jesus came for you too. Look to His cross like Nathan did and let not your hearts be troubled. Believe in God; believe also in Jesus, your Savior who died for you. Boast in your weakness like Nathan.

So, that is the *first* reason why Nathan can boast even in the weakness of his death: it provides the opportunity for all of you to hear the Good News of Jesus Christ today. And what a thought that is! Nathan is still confessing the Gospel of Jesus Christ even at his own funeral!

Then there is the other reason that Nathan can boast even in the weakness of his death. The reason that tells you *why* the Gospel of Jesus gave him such hope. And why it gives certain hope to *you* and *all who believe*. And that is this truth: *Jesus has given Nathan eternal life just as He promised*. Right now, Nathan's soul is in Paradise with Jesus. And what's more, because Jesus lives, because our Redeemer is raised from the dead, so too Nathan will live in his body. That body of his which is sown in weakness, placed into the ground a perishable body, will rise in power, an imperishable body (1 Cor. 15:42–43). So, Nathan, even as I speak, is boasting in heaven in the weakness of his death, knowing full well that our Lord's power is made perfect in weakness, and his body will rise again to be with all of you who trust in our Lord Jesus Christ.

Nathan had practice with this defiance of death here on earth. That hymn we sang just before the sermon was his practice. Listen again to what Nathan sang many times with you, Ashley, Lily and Noah, and with our congregation here at Trinity. Imagine Nathan smiling and saying:

> Death, you cannot end my gladness:
> I am baptized into Christ!
> When I die, I leave all sadness
> To inherit paradise!
> Though I lie in dust and ashes
> Faith's assurance brightly flashes:
> Baptism has the strength divine
> To make life immortal mine.
> There is nothing worth comparing
> To this lifelong comfort sure!
> Open-eyed my grave is staring;

Even there I'll sleep secure.
Though my flesh awaits its raising,
Still my soul continues praising:
I am baptized into Christ;
I'm a child of paradise!

Yes, Nathan can look death in the eye as a baptized Christian, and say with Job:

I know that my Redeemer lives,
and at the last he will stand upon the earth.
And after my skin has been thus destroyed,
yet in my flesh I shall see God,
whom I shall see for myself,
and my eyes shall behold, and not another.

Nathan can boast in the weakness of his death because Jesus is faithful to His promises. Nathan can say to the weakness of death: "My Lord's power is made perfect in weakness. I saw it all my life. And now I see it in my death, too." Nathan can say, "Death cannot separate me from my God, from Ashley, from Lily, from Noah, from my parents, my siblings, my friends, or anyone who trusts in Jesus Christ, who has defeated death for us all!"

You see, then, how Nathan's weakness is actually his strength. *And so is yours.* Today you cry tears. You cry tears because you miss a Christian man who packed so much love for you into his short life. Ashley, you cry tears because Nathan was such a self-giving, Christlike husband for you and you will miss him dearly. Lily and Noah, you cry tears because your dad loved you like your heavenly Father does, and you will miss his kindness toward you. Kevin and Deb, you cry tears because you know that your son's life exuded the love of God's Son, flowing from his faith in the one who loved him and gave Himself for him. I cry tears because I will miss him for the encouragement he was for me. You, Nathan's wife, his children, his parents, his siblings, his in-laws, his friends, his loved-ones whom he loved because God first loved him, your tears might look like weakness. But consider how your Lord cried tears too, *yet said,*

"I am the resurrection and the life. He who believes in Me will live, even though he dies; and whoever lives and believes in Me will never die." (Jn 11:25–26)

This means Jesus not only sympathizes with you and all who believe in Him, *but He promises that He will one day wipe away all your tears from your faces.* He will raise *you too* from your weakness. So, you too can boast like Nathan. For Jesus will bring you into His Father's house where He has prepared a place for you with Nathan. And you will see him again. And you will embrace him again. And you will live in perfect love with him forever with our Lord.

Until that great day, the grace of our Lord is sufficient for you. His power is made perfect in weakness. For Nathan. For you. For all who believe in Jesus as the way, the truth, and the life.

In Jesus' Name. **Amen.**

SERMON 5.

"Meet Virginia, Meet Jesus"

(1 Thessalonians 4:13–18)

Dear family of Virginia, dear friends, dear brothers and sisters in Christ:

Grace, mercy, and peace to you from God our Father
and our Lord Jesus Christ. **Amen.**

Back in the late nineties there was a pop song called "Meet Virginia." And whether I wanted it to happen or not, I would get this song stuck in my head when visiting Virginia Bahr. She is the first Virginia I met, so the line in the song, "I can't wait to meet Virginia…" periodically rang in my ears as I went to see her. And it was true. I *did* look forward to *meet Virginia* over the years. First at church, then her house, then her assorted rooms over at the Lutheran Home.

And, of course, you, her family, couldn't wait to *meet Virginia* for an array of get-togethers, too. Because she was a faithful family member, a devoted mother and grandmother who made sure she was there for all sorts of your special events across the decades. She clearly loved you all. The prominently displayed wall of pictures of her grandchildren that she had for years in her room proved that well enough. She used to look at the photos and talk about you, about how she prayed for you and your Christian faith, about when she last saw you or when she was going to see you again. So, it was clear that Virginia loved meeting up with her children and grandchildren and great-grandchildren, and other family, and no doubt, that you loved to *meet Virginia* too.

For us at Trinity, meeting her was a joy, as well. The children would *meet Virginia* at Sunday and Midweek School, which she graciously taught for years. Her fellow singers would *meet Virginia* for choir practice as they gave glory to God through their voices. Many of the women of the congregation would *meet Virginia* for the Lutheran Women's Missionary League Bible

Studies and gatherings. And the faithful, of course, would *meet Virginia* at church as she regularly heard God's Word as a child, with Elwyn, then her whole family, then by herself, then over at the Lutheran Home services and shut-in calls these last several years.

This last part, to *meet Virginia* as we gathered around our Lord's Word, was *the* most important part of her life. It is the most important part of *every* Christian's life. Because this is how Virginia and all the faithful came to *meet Jesus*, our Good Shepherd. And this was so important because if Virginia did <u>not</u> meet Jesus and have Him as her Good Shepherd, she would have remained a wandering sheep. And the same is true of all of us. "All we like sheep have gone astray," Isaiah reminds us, "we have turned—every one—to his own way." (Isaiah 53:6) That's what sin is. Sin is not just doing a few things wrong here and there. No, sin is to turn and walk away from God. Sin is to choose *your* way instead of *His* way. What's worse, unless we *meet Jesus*, our Good Shepherd, we would *remain* as lost lambs, sinners headed to *death*. The devil would devour us like a wolf does a defenseless sheep in an exposed pasture, and we would perish eternally along with him. Yes, and that *would have* happened to Virginia, too, *had she not come to* <u>meet Jesus.</u>

So, it is indisputable that *the* most important part of Virginia's life was that she gathered around the Lord's Word to *meet Jesus*, our Good Shepherd. Jesus tells us specifically what it means for *her* and for *all* of the sheep of His fold to *meet Him*. Again, He says:

> My sheep hear my voice, and I know them, and they follow me. *I give them eternal life*, and they will never perish, and no one will snatch them out of my hand. My Father, who has given them to me, is greater than all, and no one is able to snatch them out of the Father's hand.

Jesus *is* the Good Shepherd, who takes wandering sheep and calls them to be His own. He calls out with His voice, that is with His Word, saying, "Stay close to Me, and I will protect you from sin, death, and the devil. I will <u>give</u> you eternal life and you need never worry, because I and My heavenly Father, who is more powerful than all, have you in the firm grasp of our hand." And the sheep of Jesus, the Good Shepherd, hear this glorious Word of His and believe it. *Virginia* heard this Word and believed it; she listened to this voice of her Good Shepherd throughout her life and trusted that there she would *meet Jesus* and be safe from harm.

Yes, Virginia trusted that Jesus knew her. That He knew her because He took all her sins upon Himself and died for them. He let that wolf, the devil, devour *Him* on the cross. But He died to *defeat* the devil. He rose triumphant, the victor over sin, death, *and* the devil for Virginia, for you, and for the whole world. This is how it works: the devil's power is to lead the world into sin, to make us wander like sheep after *him* into death and hell. But Jesus defeated that power. Now, He forgives our sins by virtue of His death in our place. Now, He gives us eternal life as a gift that the devil cannot steal from Him and those who cling to Him. Now, heaven is the future of all who follow Him, that is who listen to His voice and trust in Him to the end.

All of this is the certain truth for *Virginia*. She *is* a sheep of the Good Shepherd. She *did* listen to His voice and *trusted* in Him from the beginning of her life to the very end so that her soul now dwells in heaven. I *know* this because I was privileged to preach Jesus' Word to her even up to the last day of her earthly life. Virginia would confess her sin, receive forgiveness, declare that Jesus is her Good Shepherd who laid down His life for her and took it up again. She took comfort that the Lord is her Shepherd who led her to the still waters of Holy Baptism and made her His sheep. She rejoiced that He prepared a table for her where she received His body and blood to nourish her body and soul until she reached the green pasture of Paradise. Virginia would come to *meet Jesus*, trusting in His Word, and for *this reason* her soul got to *meet Jesus* face to face when she died.

And if *you* would like to *meet Virginia* again, *meet Jesus* yourselves. His voice rings out not just *today*. His voice *continues* to ring out from pulpits like this one week in and week out. His voice is still calling wandering sheep to join or rejoin the fold. To stop walking *away* from God according to your own standards but *toward* the Good Shepherd who shows you the better way. To follow Him. Because His voice is saying to you, "I am *your* Good Shepherd, too. I laid down My life for *you*, as well. All your sin, whatever it is, I took upon Myself and paid for it so that you are forgiven fully and freely in Me. The devil I defeated *for* you. Eternal life I give *to* you. Trust that this is for *you* too," Jesus' voice still rings out. "Follow Me by clinging to the promise of your Baptism which says that you are a white-wooled sheep of the Good Shepherd, that is righteous and holy in God's sight through faith in your Good Shepherd. Join My flock in regularly feeding on My Words in the pasture of My Church," Jesus bids all of you today.

And all who hear this voice of Jesus in faith have the gift of eternal life and will *meet Virginia* again. In *heaven*, yes, where her soul rejoices right now with Elwyn and all the saints and angels. But *also* on the Last Day, when this body of hers right here that has fallen asleep will awaken. She has died in Christ, which means that when He returns, Virginia's body will rise to immortality with all the faithful of every generation. And all who trust in the Good Shepherd who are still alive will *also* be changed in an instant to have immortal bodies themselves. And then, St. Paul informs us, we will all "be caught up together with them in the clouds to *meet the Lord* in the air, and so we will always be with the Lord." What a glorious future the flock of the Good Shepherd has! We will *meet Virginia* again just as surely as we will *meet Jesus*. "Therefore encourage one another with these words."

In Jesus' Name. **Amen.**

SERMON 6.

"The Most Significant Day of George's Life"

(ROMANS 6:3–5)

Dear family of George, especially you Pauline, dear friends, dear brothers and sisters in Christ:

Grace, mercy, and peace to you from God our Father and our Lord Jesus Christ. **Amen.**

G EORGE TOLD ME the other week that the most significant day of his life was December 7, 1941. We all know that day as the attack on Pearl Harbor, which subsequently got the United States involved in World War II. But that day was significant to George in *another* way. Because on the day that the enemies of our country decimated the U.S. Pacific Fleet in the waters of Pearl Harbor, our almighty God destroyed the power of *George's* enemies—sin, death, and the devil—in the waters of Holy Baptism.

And that needed to happen for George. It was *because* that happened that we know George as a Christian man. As a loving husband of over 53 years. A faithful father and grandfather. A man who did so much in his various roles for this congregation throughout his lifelong membership here, not to mention all the support he gave to missions throughout the world too. Yes, we know him as George, the Christian farmer who loved his family and the land and the fields and the God who caused them to grow and increase for him for decades through good days and bad. But the *reason* George showed this love and dedication that we know him for is because George knew the love of God in Christ Jesus *first*. George knew that God poured this love upon him in his Baptism into Christ's death and resurrection. Yes, George knew he needed that Baptism to happen. And he cherished the day that it did.

Why? Because George believed that he was a sinner who could do nothing about it. George knew that the wages of sin is death and he could do nothing about that either, which our presence here today confirms. George knew that unless he had a Savior, unless God did something about his dire, serious situation, there was only punishment in his future when he eventually reached the other side and met God face to face. And George knew that was true of everyone out there, too, you and me included.

So, George cherished his Baptism. Yes, while the country remembered the enemy who attacked us, each December 7th, George was able to remember each year that God attacked *his* enemies and overcame them for him. Because that's what God does in Holy Baptism. And He does so by uniting us through Baptism to Christ's *death*. The death that Christ died once for all, to bear our guilt and suffer our punishment for our sin. The death whereby Christ atoned for our every sin when He offered His righteous life in exchange for our sinful ones. The death that took the place of *our* death and stripped the devil of his power to take us to hell. Yes, in Holy Baptism God says to us, and He said to George, "I cover your sin with the righteousness of Christ. I wash your sins away with His blood. I join you to His death and personally apply to you everything that His death accomplished: forgiveness of sin, victory over the devil, and the defeat of death itself."

So, George cherished his Baptism. And he cherished it also because in it God unites us to Christ's *resurrection* too. Pearl Harbor woke the country up to our enemies. And Baptism wakes us up to our *spiritual* ones. Sin and Satan try to rule over us our whole life through and take us with them into death and hell. But George cherished his Baptism throughout his life because he knew that in it he had *new life* in Christ. Every *day* George rose to that new life, drawing strength from the resurrection of Christ that he had victory over his enemies. Every *week* George rose to that new life, as he came to Trinity throughout his decades to confess his sins, receive forgiveness, and strengthen his faith through his Savior's promises. And this new life produced that *love* in George that you knew so well. That love that you enjoyed was the fruit of his faith in *God's love for him in His Son, our Savior, Jesus Christ*. And God's love in Christ produced *hope* in George too. A certainty that just as Christ rose from the dead, so too would George, who trusted in Him. George cherished his Baptism because it united him to Christ's resurrection, promising him eternal life in body and soul.

We know that he *has* that eternal life now in his *soul*. I know it so *certainly* too. Few times have I been so privileged to see a man so clearly confess his Christian faith to the very end. But I was privileged to see it in George. When he finally could not come here to the church which he called home all his life, he asked me to come out to the house that he called home for the last thirty years with Pauline. There, where many meals with family were shared, he shared in the foretaste of the feast to come in the Lord's Supper. When no procedure or medicine could heal him, he looked to the healing medicine of immortality in his Savior's Body and Blood, trusting that when his days on earth ceased, he would depart in peace to his Lord. And he did.

And last week, when I came out to the house to commend his soul into our heavenly Father's hands, I and the family gathered heard George give as hearty "Amens!" as his feeble voice could muster to all of God's promises in Christ. And as I sang "Abide with Me," which we will sing again today, and "God Loved the World, So that He Gave," George could not help but sing along. Though his eyes were closed and his body weak, his faith was strong and his heart was open to all of the promises his Savior gave him when he was baptized. And George believed it all and was saved. And those of us present were privileged to witness it right before the angels finally ushered George's *soul* to Paradise, where he lives right now, singing strongly with the angelic hosts in heaven.

And his *body* right here, we lay to rest today. In the sure and certain hope that Jesus will raise it from the dead. That He will reunite George's soul with *this* body and glorify it on the day He returns. So that though George has died, yet shall he live *just as Jesus promised*. United by Baptism to Jesus' death and resurrection, believing in his Savior, who is the resurrection and the life, this death of George will lead to his resurrection too. So that all who follow in the faith like George will embrace him again in the life that never ends.

To that end, embrace the most significant day of *your* life too. No, you might not be able to say that something written in the history books happened on the day *you* were baptized like George could. But you *can* say that something was written in the *Book of Life* that day. *Your name*. That is why the day of George's Baptism was *really* so significant. Not just because it was a day to remember for our *country*. But because it was a day to remember for *eternity*. And so it is for you too who believe and are baptized. "When nothing else revives your soul, / Your Baptism stands and makes you whole /

And then in death completes you," as the hymn puts it. That is to say, the promises of Baptism stand for you to return to in faith *daily*, *weekly*, until the day *you* die. Yes, Christ's death and resurrection is for *you* too. His victory over sin, death, and the devil are *yours*. So, like George, cherish this. Cherish that you are united to your Savior, who defeated all your enemies for you. Cherish your Savior's precious promises by dying to sin and rising to new life like George did, strengthening your faith by hearing this Gospel truth regularly in church until the day you enter glory like George and finally reach the resurrection of all flesh.

Then you will see like George did how significant a day December 7, 1941 *really* was. And how significant the day *you* were baptized was too. Because like George and Job you know that your Redeemer lives, and at the last He will stand upon the earth. And after your skin has been thus destroyed, yet in your flesh you shall see God, beholding Him with your own eyes. Yes, on that day, when all your mourning ceases and your tears are wiped away, you will see clearly that December 7, 1941 was a day of victory for God's dear child George. And that the day of *your* Baptism was as well.

In Jesus' Name. **Amen.**

SERMON 7.

"Death Swallowed Up for Arlene"

(1 Corinthians 15:51–57)

Alleluia! Christ is risen! **He is risen, indeed! Alleluia!**

Dear family of Arlene, dear friends, dear brothers and sisters in Christ:

"Death is swallowed up in victory." What a mystery this is that St. Paul gives us! You'll hear of people swallowing *food*. My son, for example, loved to swallow the zucchini bread Arlene used to make, always excited when she sent a loaf home after my visit with her. And many of us got to swallow down the garden produce she so happily and dutifully tended for so many years. Or the fish caught up at Nestor Falls in Canada. And you'll hear of people swallowing something to drink, too. Arlene, for example, when asked the secret to her long life said she drank down a beer a day and laughed a lot. So from food and drink we understand swallowing. But *death*? "*Death* is swallowed up in victory"? What a mystery for us to think upon today!

Now, to understand this mystery and how it applies to Arlene, we must consider a couple of things. First is that death happens because of sin. "The sting of death is sin," we just heard. And elsewhere we read, "The wages of sin is death." Scripture is clear as day on this dark truth. Since the devil led Adam and Eve into sin, they died. And so every human being has inherited this original sin and has died because of it. Were it not for sin there would be no death. So, the reason we will die is due to our sin. The reason Arlene died is due to her sin.

The second thing we must consider is that "the power of sin is the law," as we just heard. And elsewhere we read that "through the law comes the knowledge of sin." So, a person can deny sin all they want but we know of our sin because God gives us this knowledge through His law. His law is to love Him above all things and to love your neighbor above yourself. And His law has the power to expose our hearts and lives as those that do not love God as we should, that do not love our neighbors perfectly as God's law demands.

So, to understand the mystery of death being swallowed up in victory and how this applies to Arlene we must know these truths first. Arlene knew them well. "The sting of death is sin, and the power of sin is the law… *But thanks be to God, who gives us the victory through our Lord Jesus Christ." Arlene knew this all the more!* She knew that God gives us the victory because His Son, Jesus Christ, took all our sin upon Himself. God gives us the victory because His Son, Jesus Christ, became man and fulfilled God's Law for us and died for us, swallowing God's wrath against our sin down to the bitter dregs. God gives us the victory because His Son, Jesus Christ, raised Himself to life and swallowed up death for Himself.

And now, Jesus gives that victory—eternal life—to all who listen to His voice. Arlene listened to His voice, the voice of her Good Shepherd. He guided her to swallow down more than just the food she planted in plenty in the garden *and well into her nineties!* More than that, He guided her to swallow down the victory He won for her: to believe the Good News of Jesus Christ as her Savior from sin and death and hell. By faith Arlene drank down this truth regularly throughout her life. Whenever I saw her in her house she confessed her sin and heard the voice of her Good Shepherd: that He had laid down His life for her and forgives her. That He baptized Her into His death and resurrection and gave her a new life. She would listen intently to sermons preaching this truth and swallow it down. And she would also swallow down the Lord's Supper, Christ's body and blood given and shed for her, and trust that He had won the victory for her. That Jesus swallowed up her death for her forever.

Yes, it is a mystery that Arlene believed: that through Jesus "Death is swallowed up in victory." This means that Arlene is not dead but sleeping, just as St. Paul says. Yes, her soul is rejoicing in heaven with Jesus and Virgil and all the saints. But her body here is sleeping. And when Jesus returns, "in a moment, in the twinkling of an eye, at the last trumpet . . . the dead will be raised imperishable," as Scripture says. The bodies of all who listened to the voice of the Good Shepherd will be changed to be like His glorious body. And when this happens, when the perishable body puts on the imperishable, and this mortal body puts on immortality, "then shall come to pass the saying that is written: 'Death is swallowed up in victory.'" Then we shall see Arlene alive again, along with all who believed in our Lord Jesus.

Yes, "Death is swallowed up in victory." What a mystery this is that St. Paul gives us! And what a comfort for all who believe in our Lord, Jesus Christ. Especially for her family, whom she loved so much and talked about with such joy. Believe this: "Death is swallowed up in victory" for Arlene. You'll hear of people swallowing zucchini bread and beer. And it'll give you a smile. But to swallow this truth gives more than just a momentary satisfaction. It removes the sting of death and it gives eternal victory. Victory that belongs to Arlene. Victory that belongs to all of you who listen to the voice of Jesus, the Good Shepherd, and believe on His name.

Alleluia! Christ is risen! **He is risen, indeed! Alleluia!**

SERMON 8.

"No More Moving"

(JOHN 14:1–6)

Dear family of Pat, dear friends, dear brothers and sisters in Christ:

Grace, mercy, and peace to you from God our Father
and our Lord Jesus Christ. **Amen.**

NO MORE MOVING. Moving seemed to be a theme for Pat's life, didn't it? From Ossian, Iowa, to Postville, to Norfolk, Virginia, then back to Iowa in Maquoketa, then Preston, then Whittemore, then LaPorte City, then Wilton, then Vinton. And I suppose she got a breather for a little while here… But then came the tornado of 2016 which forced Pat to move from her apartment to Kevin and Betty's briefly to Dysart to Ridgeway Place to Bridges to Western Home to a new room there not once but a few times. I probably missed a move or two in the midst of her long life, too. But *now*, *finally*, no more moving. Pat is home. Her *soul* is in heaven.

But *why* is Pat home? Did *she* prepare the home in heaven herself? Or did she *receive* it because of the preparation of *someone else*? Listen again to the words of Jesus:

> "Let not your hearts be troubled. Believe in God; believe also in me. In my Father's house are many rooms. If it were not so, would I have told you that I go to prepare a place for you? And if a I go and prepare a place for you, I will come again and will take you to myself, that where I am you may be also."

Jesus prepared a place for Pat in His Father's house. *Jesus* is the reason that Pat is home in heaven and why *anyone else* goes there too. Yes, *Jesus* prepared this place for Pat in His Father's house with nails and wood, blood, sweat, and tears … but not in the way we usually think. The nails Jesus used were the nails that pierced Him. The wood that Jesus used was the cross on which

He died. The blood, sweat, and tears came flowing out from Jesus because of the suffering He went through. For Pat. For you. For the whole world.

You see, Jesus died for our sin. All of it. And without this death of Jesus, there is no room prepared for *anyone but Him* in the Father's house. Because Jesus is God's Son from eternity. He has always dwelled with His Father. The house is already built from before the foundation of the world. But *none of us* could enter unless our sin is taken away. God will not allow sin to pollute His perfect house. *But* because He is love, He still wants us there. He wants Pat there. So, in the fulness of time, God sent forth His only Son to prepare a place for Pat and for all of us in His Father's house. He, the perfect Son of God, took on our flesh and blood from the Virgin Mary. He lived a perfect life in our place. And He gave that life to God in exchange for our sinful lives. On the cross, He paid the price for our every sin by suffering the death we deserve. On the cross, God counted Him the sinner, in order that He might credit to us Jesus' perfect, righteous life. Yes, on the cross, Jesus, God's Son, prepared a place in His Father's house for Pat, for you, for me, for all sinners who live, have lived, or ever will live.

And you *benefit* from this when you receive this truth in faith. And this faith in Him is a gift too. Jesus said that after He goes and prepares a place for you, He will come again and take you to Himself, that where He is you may be also. Jesus is risen from the dead and He has sent forth the Holy Spirit into this world, who works through this Word that you are hearing now to create faith in Jesus. And when you have faith in Jesus, clinging to His precious Word, Jesus is with you. And He is guiding you on the way to the Father's house. Because He *is* the *Way*. He is the *Truth* that gives you knowledge of salvation. He is the *Life* who grants you eternal life as a free gift, purchased by His blood. All who receive this truth in faith, all who cling to Jesus and His Spirit-filled Word by faith, they are children of God. And Jesus is guiding them through life *and* through death to be with Him in His Father's house forever.

I *know* that this is the case for Pat. I *know* that Pat believed in Jesus throughout her life, throughout every move. I *know* this because for the last ten years I have proclaimed this Gospel of Jesus Christ to Pat here in this church, then in her apartment here in Vinton, then after the tornado briefly at Kevin and Betty's, at Ridgeway Place, at Bridges, at the Western Home—all of the rooms there, too! Surrounded by more cardinals than you can count, Pat would confess her sin and cling by faith to the forgiveness Jesus won for her. Pat would confess her faith in her Father in heaven, who created her; His Son, who prepared a place for her in her Father's house by His death on the cross; and the Holy Spirit, who brought her into the communion of saints and made her a child of God through her Baptism into Christ. And Pat would also receive Christ's body and blood for her forgiveness, after which I would see her anxiety melt away for a moment as her heart was not troubled or afraid. Yes, and Pat would sing with me of Jesus, talk to me about Jesus, confess Jesus as her Savior. So, I *know* that there is no more moving for Pat. Jesus has guided her home to her fatherland in heaven.

And if *you* want a place in the Father's house like Pat, trust in Jesus yourself. Be a part of a church that proclaims Jesus purely, since He is with you in His Spirit-filled Word and Sacrament and keeps you in the faith through these precious means of grace. And if you need help with finding a church home around here, I happen to know of one here in Vinton located on East 13th Street. Because you need this Word of Jesus to keep you in the faith if you want to see Pat again. Sin is real. It's why we die. But you do not need to die *in sin*. You can die *with Christ*, who took your sin away. You can rise with Him to newness of life. You can receive the free forgiveness that He purchased for you. You can be baptized into Him and cling to the promise that you are God's own child through faith in Him and an heir according to the hope of eternal life. What is for Pat is for you too. It is a gift. It is God's desire for you all. "He who did not spare His own Son but gave him up for us all, how will he not also with him graciously give us all things." He is so gracious. So loving. So, let not *your* hearts be troubled either. Believe in God; believe also in Jesus who prepared a place for *you* too in His Father's house…

That's where Pat is. Pat is home. At least, her *soul* is. Her *body* right here awaits the resurrection. And we do not want to gloss over that. Because it is such a wonderful and comforting truth and promise. One day Jesus will return in *His* body to raise *all* bodies. And those whose souls are with Him in heaven, including Pat's, and those who trust in Him here on earth, will rise with immortal bodies just like our Lord's. On that day, our Lord will swallow up death forever and wipe away tears from all the faces who rejoice in His appearing. Including Pat's. Right now, we can only *imagine* how much joy Pat's soul has in heaven. But on *that* day of resurrection, we will not need to *imagine* Pat's face. We who continue in the faith like she did will *see* it. Her mouth will be full of pearly white teeth. Her hair like when she was in her teens. Her countenance anxiety-free. Her hands as steady as a surgeon. Her whole body youthful. Her eyes gazing at her Savior in thanksgiving for all He has done for us. And we will also hear her pleasant voice blending in with the angels and saints of all ages, including her husband Rick's and our own.

So, while we will miss Pat in *this life*, we rejoice amidst our tears in the *eternal* life given to her and to us by Jesus, who is the Way, the Truth, and the *Life*. *He* has prepared it so that for Pat there is no more moving. Just rejoicing as she dwells in the house of the Lord forever.

In Jesus' Name. **Amen.**